SELECTED READINGS FROM

MARTIN
*L*UTHER

EDITED WITH INTRODUCTION BY
ROBERT VAN DE WEYER

Fleming H. Revell Company
Tarrytown, New York

Fleming H. Revell Company Publishers,

Tarrytown, New York

Copyright © 1991 Hunt & Thorpe
Text © 1991 by Robert van de Weyer
Originally published in the UK by Hunt and Thorpe 1991
First published in North America by Fleming Revell
ISBN 0-8007-7132-X

Illustrations by
Fred Apps, James Barton, Elvira Dadd and Vic Mitchell

Manufactured in the United Kingdom.

1 2 3 4 5 6 7 – 96 95 94 93 92 91

CONTENTS

INTRODUCTION

*H*is critics have compared Luther with a volcano: his fiery sermons and books erupted over Europe, generating more heat than light. Yet today many of his most ardent admirers are Roman Catholics who believe that if he had lived in the twentieth century, far from being excommunicated by the Pope, he would have been hailed as a saint. It is impossible to be neutral about Luther: either you are inspired by the sheer passion of his faith and his uncompromising honesty; or you recoil from the stubborn arrogance of a man who preferred to split the Church asunder rather than to change one jot of his theology. Many of his ideas, so controversial in his day, are now taken for granted by Protestants and Catholics alike. Yet the continuing fascination of Luther is that the theology which formed the basis of the Reformation was not the product of quiet intellectual reflection, but emerged from an intense spiritual struggle within the heart of this emotional man. He never indulged in theological speculation, but constantly related his insights to his own experience.

Martin Luther was born on November 10th, 1483 near Mansfeld, in the center of Germany's major mining area. His father, Hans, was a miner, and in his early years Martin endured considerable hardship. But Hans possessed the same unflagging zeal that Martin was to inherit, and within a decade had become the owner of several smelting furnaces, so that in his teenage years Martin belonged to the wealthy elite of the town. The atmosphere at home was one of high-minded piety, and Martin in later life complained of his coldness of relationships within the family. At university in Erfurt, Martin shone as a brilliant debater and public speaker, as well as a fine musician; and his father entertained ambitious hopes for him in a professional career. But at the age of 21, as he was walking near Erfurt, he was suddenly grasped by the conviction that God wanted him to be a monk – an event he later vividly described. To his father's horror he entered the Augustinian monastery at Erfurt where he turned his incisive mind to the study of theology; and within four years, by 1509, was himself giving lectures to new monks.

The Augustinian order that Luther had joined was extremely strict, and Luther was punctilious in following every letter of its rule. He was soon undertaking long fasts, and devoting many extra hours to private prayer; and he recorded every minor lapse, in order to beg forgiveness at his weekly confession. But the harder he tried to please God by such rigid discipline, the more troubled his soul became. His sense of guilt grew rather than diminished, and each new effort at self-mortification only deepened his inner torment. As he himself wrote, he began to hate God as an unjust judge, who could never be appeased. His own health began to deteriorate, and he suffered from chronic insomnia and constipation.

Peace finally came, after fourteen tortured years, through meditating on the phrase in Paul's Epistle to the Romans, "the righteousness of God." It struck him with the force of revelation that righteousness could not be won by human effort, but was a free and unmerited gift from God. Thus the harsh life within the monastery was in vain unless he could open his heart to God to receive this gift. For the first time in his life he felt true joy as the burden of guilt was lifted from his shoulders.

This private spiritual experience was the inspiration of the Protestant Reformation, which within less than a decade was shaking the whole of Europe. He developed the doctrine, which became the corner stone of his teaching, of "justification by faith alone": the individual is "justified" before God, not through any "good works" but by receiving the gift of faith from God; good works, in particular acts of love towards one's neighbor, are the natural expression of faith, but do not of themselves save a person's soul. He thus came to regard the prevailing teaching in the Catholic Church as fundamentally flawed. The Pope and his bishops, in Luther's view, laid all sorts of moral obligations on the people, the greatest of which was to give generously to the church, with the promise of a spiritual reward in heaven. To Luther this reduced God and his saving power to a mere tool in the hands of the Church.

The first great controversy was over the role of "indulgences," in which the Church sold at a high price certificates that reduced the time that a person would spend after death in purgatory being punished for their sins. This long-standing abuse had gained extra momentum through the Pope's desire to build a huge new cathedral in Rome, requiring large sums from throughout Europe. To Luther it epitomized all that was wrong in the church, and he began to write long and furious letters to those in Germany promoting indulgences, especially to the Archbishop of Mainz who was also using the money raised to pay off his own debts. Then on October 31, 1517 he made his first public declaration, pinning Ninety-five Theses on the door of the church at Wittenberg, which spelt out in detail his objection to indulgences. These theses were widely circulated throughout Germany, and Luther himself was astonished at the popular support he won. The Pope himself received a copy, and ordered Luther to be tried for heresy; and, after a complex series of ecclesiastical trials, the Pope in 1520 condemned Luther's teaching, giving him sixty days to retract on pain of excommunication and imprisonment.

Luther refused, and in 1521 the Pope sent a letter to the emperor of Germany calling on him to arrest Luther. The emperor refused, and instead summoned a council, the Diet of Worms, where Luther would have an opportunity to answer the charges for himself. Luther's books were laid on a table, and he was asked to revoke their contents. In his robust reply he did not defend his views, but challenged the Diet to find any error within his writings. The Diet did not respond, but nonetheless eventually passed an edict pronouncing that Luther had "departed from the Christian way." By now, however, the great majority of the German people were behind Luther, and, much against his own will, he was regarded as the champion of their deep resentment of Rome. Luther's friends feared that the Pope's supporters might assassinate him, and he was forced into hiding at Wurtburg castle, where he began to translate the Bible into German.

Luther realized that healing the rift with Rome was impossible, and he now set about constructing a new

reformed church. Already in 1520 he had written two public letters, which were in effect manifestos of the Reformation. In them he expressed his belief that all Christians are "priests," in direct contact with God through the Holy Spirit and thus able to interpret the Scriptures for themselves. So the claims of the Pope and his bishops and priests to be the exclusive mediators of God's grace and truth to the people were false. After his return to the public arena Luther preached countless sermons, and published a stream of letters and pamphlets, on every aspect of church life. He defined the basic doctrines of Protestant belief, he specified the functions of the ordained ministry, and he constantly stressed the central role of the Bible.

Sadly the reformed church was soon suffering division within itself, with the radicals wanting to cast aside all traditions in the hope of recreating the pristine Christianity of the apostolic Church. Luther regarded such an aim as delusory, and was a staunch defender of many Catholic traditions within worship and teaching. The greatest challenge, however, was not religious but political. The stress within Protestant doctrine on individual liberty before God prompted many peasants to seek liberty from their feudal masters, and at the end of 1524 they rose up in revolt, supported by a number of Protestant ministers.

Luther was appalled. Already he had turned his mind to political questions, and had specified the differing spheres of authority of Church and State, as well as advising Christian rulers as to how they should exercise their authority. Luther, (who, despite his religious ideas, remained conservative at heart), had little sympathy with the peasants' cause; but, more importantly, he regarded all forms of violent rebellion as morally wrong. Thus he advised the German rulers to suppress the peasants with as much force as necessary.

Until the end of his life in 1546, books and tracts, letters and sermons, continued to pour from Luther's pen, so that his complete works run to 55 volumes. Amidst the mass of material the most moving pieces are those where he expresses personal feelings, revealing a man of warmth and humor. In 1525 he married a former nun, Katherine, and his letters to her and their children show him as a devoted husband and father – and Katherine as a strong-minded woman who, perhaps alone, was able to challenge her husband's more wayward ideas.

The greatest tribute, however, that can be paid to Martin Luther is that many of his ideas are now part of the common spiritual currency of all the churches, including the Roman Catholic Church. As a leading Catholic scholar has said, "we are all Lutherans now."

1

Entering the monastery

Luther never wrote an autobiography, but sometimes referred to the events of his life to illustrate points he was making. It is thus possible to piece together the story of his early years, especially the decision to become a monk.

I am the son of a peasant. My great-grandfather, grandfather and father were peasants. I was expected to become an overseer, bailiff or some other such official, someone with authority over others.

I made the decision to become a monk while walking near Erfurt. I was struck by a flash of lightning, and I cried out in terror: "Help me, St. Anna, and I will become a monk." I was saved, and God received my promise. I soon regretted it and my friends tried to dissuade me from entering the monastery. But I stuck to it, and on the day before the feast of St. Alexis I invited my friends to a party, to bid them farewell. The next day they accompanied me to the monastery, and still tried to restrain me. But I stuck to my promise, and said to them: "Today you see me for the last time, for tomorrow I shall be dead to the world."

My father was angry at my entering the monastery and refused to give his consent. He loved me dearly and feared that my decision was rash and impetuous. His own plan for my future was that I should marry a rich and honorable lady, and for a time he was so upset that he refused to visit me. But finally he gave up his anger and submitted to God's will. When I explained to him that I had been called to the monastery by terrors from heaven, and had entered against my own desires, he replied: "May it not prove an illusion and a

deception." Those words penetrated and lodged in the depths of my soul, tempting me to believe that I had been wrong. My father also rebuked me, saying that, in entering the monastery against his wishes, I was breaking the commandment which says a child should obey his parents. Thus, he argued, my vow was not worth a straw, because in taking it I had flouted the will and authority of my parents. Those bitter words also tempted me to doubt God's call.

2

Life as a monk

After he left the monastery Luther often reflected on his life as a monk. Sometimes he looked back with wry amusement at his own strictness. But more often he remembered with horror how his severe self-discipline only increased his sense of guilt, until finally he could stand it no longer.

I was a good monk, and kept the rules of my order so strictly that I can claim: if ever man got to heaven through monasticism, I was indeed that man. All my brothers in the monastery who knew me can testify to this. I would have become a martyr through fasting, prayer, spiritual reading and other good works if I had remained a monk much longer!

I tried always to be meek and contrite, regularly confessing my sins – indeed, I often grossly exaggerated my wrongdoing – and diligently performing the penances that were prescribed. And yet my conscience was never peaceful. I constantly doubted myself, and would say to myself: "You did not do that penance correctly; you were not contrite enough." And even when I had completed the penance, I would remember other sins which I had failed to confess. So I carried a double burden of guilt. The more I tried to remedy my condition, through more abject confession and more rigoros penance, the more troubled my conscience became. I soon became terrified of my own sin. The whole world seemed right except me. God's grace seemed to shine on everyone except me. I felt I was alone as the object of God's wrath, and that I was the most miserable of men. The whole sin of Adam and Eve seemed to rest on my shoulders.

Finally my misery became intolerable. I seemed to be suffering the pains of eternal torment every hour, every minute, every second. The whole realm of hell seemed to exist within my soul, I felt as if I were inwardly being reduced to ashes. I could see no escape; I was pinned down by my own guilt.

3

The breakthrough

After fourteen years as a monk, his spirit in increasing torment, Luther suddenly found peace through meditating on St. Paul's phrase "the righteousness of God." Until then he had struggled to win the righteousness through his own efforts. Now he suddenly realized, with the force of divine revelation, that God's righteousness is itself a gift of God, through faith in Him.

*I*n 1519 I turned my mind to trying to understand the epistle of Paul to the Romans. I was filled with a great desire to enter the mind of Paul, but was held up by one word: "righteousness."

He says that the righteousness of God is revealed in the Gospel. I hated that phrase "righteousness of God," which I had been taught to interpret as the "justice" of God, whereby he punishes sinners.

I was obsessed with the sense that, although my life as a monk was beyond reproach, I was in the eyes of God a sinner. Despite all the efforts I made to be good, my conscience could never be appeased. I did not love, but hated this just God who punishes. I blasphemed silently, crying out within my heart against God. How terrible that mankind, already eternally ruined by original sin, should be crushed by the weight of the old law, and finally condemned through the Gospel. Yet even as my spirit raged against God, my mind struggled to understand what Paul really meant.

At last, as I meditated night and day, God came to my rescue. He guided me to look at the context of Paul's phrase: "the righteous shall live by faith." Suddenly I began to grasp that this righteousness of God is a gift of God, through faith. Paul is teaching us that the righteousness of God, revealed in the Gospel, is passive, bestowed upon us in Christ. As this truth dawned, I felt I was born again, and entering the very gates of paradise. Then and there the whole face of scripture changed. Now, in the same degree that I had hated the phrase "the righteousness of God," I loved the phrase – it seemed the sweetest and most joyful phrase ever written.

4

The battle against Indulgences

Underlying Luther's objections to Indulgences was the growing conviction that bishops and priests have no power to forgive sins; instead forgiveness can only be granted by God in response to inward penitence of the heart. This view became central to the entire Protestant doctrine of salvation. Luther's fiery denunciation of Indulgences brought the anger of the Church on his head, but earned him considerable popularity among the people.

TO THE ARCHBISHOP OF MAINZ

*W*ith your approval the Papal Indulgences for the rebuilding of St. Peter's in Rome are being carried through the land. I do not object to the words of those selling Indulgences, which I have not heard, but to the false meaning attached to those words by the simple folk who hear them. They believe that when they have impoverished themselves to purchase an Indulgence, they have thereby secured their salvation, with all their sins forgiven. Thus the souls which God has placed in your care, dear Father, are being led astray, and you will have to account for them to the heavenly Father.

No bishop can by such means secure the salvation of any soul. The holy apostle Paul urges each person to work out their own salvation with fear and trembling; and Jesus himself tells us that the way which leads to life is narrow. Thus I cannot be silent when I witness the Church teaching such a false doctrine as salvation through purchasing Indulgences.

How then can you allow such falsehood to be preached, which leads poor souls not to salvation but to damnation? Deeds of purity and love are infinitely more valuable than Indulgences, yet I do not hear the bishops preaching these with the same enthusiasm. Christ has nowhere commanded Indulgences to be

Christ has nowhere commanded Indulgences to be preached, but he has commissioned all his disciples to proclaim the way of love. So the bishop who fails to ensure that love is preached, and instead urges that Indulgences are sold, exposes himself to mortal danger.

From THE NINETY-FIVE THESES

1   When our Lord and Master Jesus Christ said "Repent," he meant that the whole life of believers should be one of penitence.

2   The word cannot be understood as referring to the sacrament of penance – the words of confessions and absolution – as administered by priests, but to the inward penitence of the heart.

3   The sign of inward penitence is that there are outward acts of love and kindness to others.

4   Thus so long as there is not true inward penitence of heart, the burden of sin remains.

5   Neither the Pope, nor any bishop nor priest, has any power to forgive sins, unless there is inward penitence of the heart.

6   The Pope, bishops and priests cannot forgive sins but only declare that they have been forgiven by God...

43   Christians should be taught that one who gives to the poor or lends to the needy does a better action than purchasing an Indulgence.

44   This is because love breeds love, so that acting lovingly, love will grow in a man's heart.

45   Christians should be taught that one who gives to the poor or lends to the needy does a better action than purchasing an Indulgence.

47   Christians should be taught that the Pope, bishops and priests have more need of the prayers of believers than of their money...

92   Away, then, with those preachers who say to Christ's people, "Peace, peace!" when there is no peace.

93   Good riddance to those preachers who say to Christ's people, "The cross, the cross!" when there is no cross.

94   Christians should be urged, purely and simply, to follow the way of Christ wherever it leads.

5

The manifestos of the Reformation

In 1520 Luther wrote two open letters which were in effect manifestos of the German Reformation. The first was to the Christian nobility of Germany, who already were grumbling at the financial burdens which the Roman church placed upon them. It spells out clearly Luther's doctrine of the "priesthood of all believers," in which every Christian has a spiritual ministry. The second "On Christian Liberty" is the classic Protestant statement of the individual's freedom before God.

*T*he time for silence has gone, and the time to speak has come. Thus I wish to put some points concerning the reformation of the Christian church, seeking the support of the Christian nobility of the German nation.

The distress and misery which oppresses the Christian church, especially here in Germany, have led us to God, begging that he may reach down with his hand and help his wretched people. We cannot improve matters through our own strength, but must humbly trust in God, seeking his help with earnest prayer.

The Pope and many of the bishops have built two walls around themselves to protect themselves against any reformation. Firstly they assert that their spiritual power is above all temporal power, so that they can flout the laws of the land with impunity. Secondly, if anyone attempts to rebuke them with the teaching of the Bible, they reply that they alone can interpret the meaning of the Bible.

Let us, in the first place, attack the first wall, The Pope, bishops, priests and monks describe themselves as the "spiritual estate"; while the princes, lords, artisans and peasants are called the "temporal estate." This is a dangerous and hypocritical lie. All Christians belong to the spiritual estate because all belong to the body of Christ. Christians are equal and united in baptism and in faith; they differ only in their work and office within the Church. Indeed all Christians are consecrated priests by baptism. Those who hold positions of leadership within the Church do so only by the gift of God and with the consent of the people.

To put the matter even more plainly, if a little company of pious Christian laymen were taken prisoners and carried away into a desert, and had not among them a priest consecrated by a bishop, they would not be bereft of priesthood. All are priests, and they could elect from amongst themselves leaders to perform baptisms, to preside at the mass, to declare God's absolution and to preach God's message.

It follows, therefore, that between laymen and priests, princes and bishops – that is, between the temporal and the spiritual estates, as they are called – the only real difference is one of office and function. All belong simultaneously to the spiritual and temporal estates. And all are equally subject to the laws of God and the laws of the land.

The second wall falls when the first falls. It is a wicked fable, without any foundation in the Bible itself, to claim that the Pope and bishops alone can interpret the Bible. They have taken this authority onto themselves. And, though they claim that it was given to St Peter, it is clear from St. Peter's own words that it thereby belongs to the whole Christian community. For St. Peter described us as "a royal nation, a holy priesthood."

ON CHRISTIAN LIBERTY

I begin by laying down two propositions, concerning spiritual liberty and servitude. Firstly, the Christian man is the Lord of his own life, subject to nobody. Secondly, the Christian man is the most dutiful servant of all, subject to everyone.

Man has two aspects to his nature, spiritual and physical. The spiritual aspect, which we call the soul, is the source of the new man. The physical aspect, which we call the flesh, is the old man. Thus, though flesh may wither and perish, the soul may grow in the image of Christ. As the scriptures often tell us, these two aspects may often fight against each other, the desires of the flesh opposing the needs of the soul.

Thus it is useless to decorate the body with sacred vestments, or dwell in holy places, or abstain from certain foods, because these practices only affect the body without touching the soul. Even people without faith can put on an outward display of religious devotion, in order to impress others or deceive themselves. The truth is that it does not matter what

clothes a person wears, what food he eats or where he lives. Even academic study is useless: a person can read a thousand theology books, and his soul may still not be saved.

One thing, and one thing alone, is necessary for salvation and liberty: the most holy word of God, the Gospel of Christ. The soul can do nothing without the word of God; and the soul can do without everything except the word of God. When a soul is filled with God's word, then we say that it has received faith. And the soul is saved by faith, not by any outward actions.

Faith, then, is our source of freedom. We are no longer under the yoke of the law, obliged to perform innumerable outward actions. We can freely speak and listen to God, confident of his love and guidance.

But this does not mean we reject good works. On the contrary, we should live by the highest moral standards. Once the soul is free in Christ, it will naturally express this freedom through serving the needs of others. The person who is free in Christ no longer wants to live for himself, but to live for others. From faith flow love and joy in the Lord; which makes him into a cheerful neighbor who gives without counting the cost or demanding gratitude.

Thus, though the Christian man has no outward obligation, he freely desires to take the form of a servant, as Christ did. He acts towards his neighbor as he sees God through Christ acting towards him. All this he does freely, without regard to anything except the good pleasure of God.

6

The Diet of Worms

Luther's famous speech in his defense at the Diet of Worms does not discuss the theological issues, but simply describes the nature of his writings, and then invites others to show him any errors. He compares the defense with that of Christ before the high priest. In reality it echoes that of Paul before Governor Felix, recounted in Acts 24 – possessing the same moral and spiritual power.

*M*ost serene emperor, most illustrious majesty: two questions have been put to me by your Highness, whether I acknowledged as mine the books published under my name, and whether I wished to defend or revoke their contents. I can give a plain answer to the first question, that the books published under my name are mine – although I bear no responsibility for the interpretations given to my writings.

In answer to the second question, I ask your Highness to note that my books are not all of the same kind. Some are simple expositions of faith and morals for lay-people; and even my antagonists are compelled to acknowledge that they are quite harmless, and even useful.

Another class of my writings consists of polemic against some of the doctrines of the Pope. I willingly accept that the Pope has the right, the duty even, to preach the Gospel and interpret the Scriptures. But I refute the doctrine that says that his teaching must always be correct, by virtue of his office. All doctrines

and all interpretation of the Scriptures are made by men, and hence are fallible. Indeed, the canon law upheld by the Pope even states that doctrines taught by the Pope which are contrary to the Gospel should be rejected as erroneous.

A third class of my writings has been aimed at individuals – people of consequence, as they say – who have tried to defend the Papacy and oppose my teaching. I confess that I have often been more acrimonious than befits my faith as a Christian or my

calling as a monk. But I do not pretend to be a saint, and I am not disputing about my own life but about the teaching of Christ. Thus, while I am sorry for the tone of some of these writings, I do not apologize for the contents.

I can bring no other defense to my writings than my Lord Jesus Christ brought to his own teaching, when at his interrogation before Annas he said: "If I have spoken evil, testify to the evil," If the Lord himself, who could not err, should listen to testimony against his teaching, then I, the dregs of a man, who cannot help but err, should willingly hear testimony against me. Thus if anyone at all, from the highest to the lowest, is able to convict me of error, I shall be willing, even joyful, to revoke that error. And I shall be the first to cast my books on the fire.

In the meantime, my conscience forbids me to revoke anything – and my conscience is captive to the word of God. Here I stand. I can do no other.

7

Luther's Bible

For a quarter of a century, until 1545, a year before his
death, Luther devoted much of his time to translating
the Bible into German. In the prefaces he allowed
himself to express quite personal feelings and views,
which are often both profound and revealing. The
following are extracts from these prefaces.

PREFACE TO THE OLD TESTAMENT

I beg of every pious Christian not to despise the simplicity of the language and the stories that he will find there. He should remember that, however simple the Old Testament may seem, it contains the words, works, judgments and actions of God himself. Indeed the simplicity makes fools of the wise and clever, and allows the poor and simple to see the ways of God. Therefore submit your thoughts and feelings to the stories you read, and allow yourself to be carried like a child towards God. When you become as a child your pride will melt away, and you will be like Christ himself in the stable at Bethlehem.

PREFACE TO THE NEW TESTAMENT

The Gospel of Christ is called the New Testament because it is a testament – a will in which a dying man bequeaths his property to heirs, whom he names. Christ, before his death, commanded and bequeathed this Gospel to be preached throughout the world. Thereby he gave to all who believe as their possession, everything that he had: his life, which was swallowed up in death; his righteousness, by which he gave freedom to all who believe. To us who are sinners there can be no happier news than that Christ has named us as his heirs, by choosing us as his own.

In the four gospels you find both the works and the preaching of Christ. If I had to do without one or the other, I would rather do without his works. For the works do not help me, whereas the words give life – as he himself says. John writes very little about his works, and recounts much of his preaching; while the other evangelists tell far more of his works than his words. Therefore to me John's gospel is the most precious.

PREFACE TO THE EPISTLE TO THE ROMANS

This Epistle is really the chief part of the New Testament, a bright light which illuminates the whole Bible.

Its central theme is faith. Faith is not a human achievement, won by personal effort. It is a divine work within us. In faith we are born anew in Christ. Faith is a living, busy, active, mighty thing. So the person with faith cannot help but do good works incessantly. Faith is a bold confidence in God's grace, so sure and certain that a man would stake his life on it a thousand times. This confidence makes men glad and happy in their relationships with God and with all his creatures. Through faith a man takes pleasure in obeying God's commandments; and when he has done something he will boast, not of his own abilities, but of the power of God.

8

Priests and presbyters

One of the central issues of the Reformation was the nature of ministry. Luther attacked the Roman church for ordaining "priests" who were deemed to acquire some special powers in consecrating the bread and wine at the Eucharist. To Luther "priesthood" belonged to Christ and thence to the whole Christian community. The prime task of the ordained minister, according to Luther, is preaching, for which purpose he should be trained. But he possesses no special power, and serves only with the consent of the whole community.

*T*he purpose of the ordained ministry is the preaching of God's Word. Through public preaching of the Word the Church itself is sustained, since Christianity rests on the Word of God made manifest in Christ. The Roman church has no such notion of ministry. Instead of ministers of the Word, they ordain men to offer a false sacrifice and hear empty confessions. But since it is quite certain that the mass is not a true sacrifice, and that obligatory confession is meaningless, it follows that ordination to the Roman priesthood has no divine authority. Therefore faith and conscience alike urge us to reject their ordination.

We must distinguish between "priest" and "presbyter". All Christians are priests, since a person becomes a priest by being born anew in the spirit of God. It is through the common, universal priesthood that the Church conveys the grace and love of Christ to the world – that is what priesthood means. Christ is the great high priest; and we, the body of Christ, continue his priesthood. Thus, as I say, all Christians are priests – and all priests Christian.

Let me expand this point. The traditional offices of the priest are the following: to teach, preach and proclaim the Word of God; to baptize; to administer the Eucharist; to bind and loose sins; to pray for others; to judge the doctrines and spirits of men. yet all these things are the common right of all Christians. So no man can step forward on his own authority and grasp for himself what belongs to all.

Yet the body of Christians is a community. And as a matter of good order it is necessary for the community to choose particular people to perform these various offices in the name of all. Without this provision there would be confusion. Such people must be specially educated and trained so that they can perform the offices well, to the glory of God. In particular they must be well-versed in the Scriptures, so that they may preach God's truth, not man-made inventions. These

men, chosen for office by the community, and trained for their task, are called presbyters. Thus I say that, while priests are made, presbyters are born.

What, then, is the relationship between the presbyter and the community? The presbyter is ordained by the whole community electing him at a meeting, and then laying hands upon him. He is chosen because the community sees within him the ability to nourish the community with the Word of God; and the community should pray for him that he performs the sacred offices well. But he is not infallible; being human at times he will err and preach false doctrine. At such times the community has both the right and the duty to correct him, even by calling a meeting to debate the issue at hand and to seek the Spirit's guidance. When convinced of his error, the presbyter should joyfully and willingly admit it, and undertake not to repeat it. By this means the truth of God's word is maintained.

9

The sword and the law

Many people throughout Europe felt the Church in Rome greatly overstepped its authority, enacting laws and imposing taxes beyond its proper jurisdiction. Equally many nations were oppressed by tyrannical and corrupt rulers. Thus Luther developed a clear and concise political theology, spelling out the purpose of the secular government and the limits of the Church's authority, as well as outlining the duties of a Christian king. Luther combines in a remarkable way high idealism with sturdy realism.

THE NEED FOR SECULAR GOVERNMENT

*I*f all the world were composed of real Christians, true believers, no prince, king, sword or law would be needed. Christians have in their hearts the Holy Spirit, who instructs them and causes them to wrong no one, to love everyone, and willingly and cheerfully to suffer injustice and even death for the sake of others. Thus, where every wrong is suffered and every right is done, there will be no quarrels or strife, and hence no sword or law is needed to maintain order. There is no work for the sword and the law to do amongst Christians, since they already do much more than any law demands.

But the world is not wholly composed of Christians. Those who are not Christian need laws to instruct, constrain and compel them to do what is good. A good tree does not need any teaching or law to bear good fruit, since its nature causes it to bear good fruit. A man would be a fool to make laws telling an apple tree how to bear apples and not thorns, which it is able to do far better than any man could define or direct. But a bad tree will bear bad fruit unless by law it is prevented from doing so.

Thus God has ordained that there should be a secular government, outside and beyond the Church, to pass laws and enforce those laws with the sword.

Some might be tempted to imagine that, since almost everyone is baptized as a Christian, there is no need for laws. But baptism does not of itself breed faith; and there are many who are baptized, but whose hearts are closed to faith, To loose the chains of the law would be to open the way to violence and savagery, in which people tear each other apart in pursuit of their desires.

It would be wonderful if, at some point in the future, the whole world were Christian, so that the sword could indeed be beaten into a ploughshare. But this will never happen, since the majority will always be unchristian – or, more precisely, only nominally Christian. Therefore it is impossible that there should be a common Christian government over the whole world, since the wicked outnumber the good. A man who tried to govern an entire country with the Gospel would be like a shepherd who found not only sheep in his fold, but also wolves and lions: the sheep would soon be devoured by the wolves and lions.

Thus, although Christians themselves have no need of the sword and the law, they should recognize that society as a whole needs them. They must uphold the secular government, obeying its laws, paying the taxes and levies, striving to maintain its authority. They should recognize that, just as marriage is an institution ordained by God, so also is secular government.

THE CHRISTIAN KING

The two kingdoms, of the Church and of the secular government, must be sharply distinguished. The role of the first is to encourage piety and devotion to God; and the role of the second to preserve peace and prevent evil deeds. Neither is sufficient in the world without the other, No one can become pious before God by means of the secular government. And equally peace cannot be maintained in the world by the Church.

In making this sharp distinction, we must observe the extent and limits of the authority of the government. If the king commands you to accept or reject certain doctrines, or to stop attending worship, you must say: "I owe you my obedience with my work and my goods, and in these I will follow your commands. But you cannot tell me what to believe or how to worship, for such things belong to God." The king who attempts to interfere with matters of doctrine and worship is a tyrant, and will be judged and punished as such by God.

Sadly from the beginning of the world the wise king has proved a rare bird indeed, still more the pious king. Kings have often proved to be the greatest fools or the worst knaves on earth. Therefore one must constantly expect the worst from them and look for little good from them.

Yet even if we expect the worst, we must hope for the best. Thus I urge Christian kings and princes to say to themselves: "Christ the chief ruler came and served me. He did not seek profit or honor from me, but considered only my needs, and did all he could to bring profit and honor to me. Let me do the same with my subjects, not seeking my own advantage, but their advantage, serving them through my office as Christ served me, listening to their concerns and striving to satisfy their needs." Thus a king should in his heart empty himself of his power and authority, dealing with the needs of his subjects as if they were his own needs.

When a king is in the wrong, are his people bound to obey him? I answer "No," for it is no one's duty to do wrong. Our first duty of obedience is owed to God; and where the precepts of God conflict with the decrees of the king, it is God's precepts that we must follow. What happens, then, if the subjects do not know whether the king is in the right or in the wrong? I answer that as long as they cannot know, nor find out by any possible means, the rights and wrongs of a king's decree, they may obey it without peril to their souls.

Therefore we will conclude by summarizing the fourfold duty of the Christian king. Firstly, towards God he must show unceasing devotion, asking His guidance on all matters. Secondly, towards his subjects he must show love and generosity, Thirdly, towards those who advise and counsel him, he must show an open mind and unbiased judgment. And fourthly, towards evildoers he must show firmness and courage in administering the just punishment.

10

Warning against division

From the start the new Protestant churches tended to divide into sects. This caused Luther profound grief. Faced with a split in the church at Strasburg, Luther wrote a letter reminiscent of Paul's epistle to the Corinthians on the same theme. The following is a short extract.

*S*ee to it that you do not forget what you previously were, lest you take for granted the grace and mercy you received from God, forgetting to express daily your gratitude. Remain steadfast, and constantly study the Scriptures that you may increase in knowledge of our Lord Jesus Christ. Aim always to be of one mind, and show brotherly love to one another by your actions. Thus your faith will prove itself to be real and sincere, not a worthless sham; and the devil will not return to find the house of your soul empty and swept clean for him to enter.

Above all, do not divide into sects and groups, each quarrelling with the others. When we divide into sects our attention is diverted from inward grace to outward works, each sect trying to prove its superiority over the rest. Sects arise when people set themselves up falsely as presbyters and prophets, winning allegiance not through the truth of their teaching but through their charm. Such people will always be present, ready to foster dissension, and it is for all of us to discern their falsehood and guard against them.

11

The presence of Christ

Some Protestant groups, especially those led by Zwingli, regarded the bread and wine at the Communion as simply a memorial of Christ. Luther, however, maintained the Catholic view that Christ is truly present in the bread and wine. But he added his own subtle insights about the different ways in which the mouth and the heart consume Christ's body.

When we read the accounts of the last supper in the gospels, it is clear that Christ gives his body to eat when he distributes the bread. On this we take our stand, and we believe and teach that we take to ourselves Christ's body truly and physically. But how this takes place and how Christ is present within the bread is a mystery, beyond our understanding. We should simply believe God's Word without setting bounds or measure to it. We see the bread with our eyes, but hear with our ears that Christ's body is present.

The bread which we eat is thus both physical and spiritual. The mouth eats the body of Christ physically, for it cannot grasp or eat the words, nor does it know what it is eating. Our sense of taste tells us that the mouth is eating something quite different from Christ's body, namely bread. But the heart grasps the words in faith and eats spiritually just as the mouth eats physically; and the heart knows that it is consuming Christ's body. How does it know this? It knows it through the words of Christ himself, "Eat, this is my body."

There is only one body of Christ, which both mouth and heart eat, each in its own manner. The heart cannot eat it physically nor can the mouth eat it spiritually. So God arranges that the mouth eats physically for the heart, and the heart eats spiritually for the mouth. Thus both are satisfied and saved by one and the same food.

12

Luther's Creed

Luther composed his creed in 1529 to assist teachers
in instructing people in the faith. Doctrinally it is no
different from the traditional creeds. But it possesses
a simplicity and an earthiness which are the marks of
all Luther's writings.

THE FATHER

I believe that God has created me and all other creatures. He has given to me, and preserves for me, body and soul, eyes and ears, my limbs, my reason and all my senses. Daily he bestows upon me clothes and shoes, meat and drink, house and home, wife and children, fields and cattle, and all my goods. He supplies in abundance all my bodily needs, protects me from all danger, and defends me from all evil. All this he does out of pure fatherly goodness, without any merit or worthiness on my part. And so I am bound to thank and praise him, and to serve and obey him.

THE SON

I believe that Jesus Christ, born of the Father and born of the Virgin Mary, is both God and man. He has redeemed me, who was lost and damned, delivering me from all my sins, from death, and from the power of the devil. He did this not with gold and silver as a ransom, but with his holy and precious blood, shed for me on the cross. Thus I now belong to him, and will live together with him in his kingdom for all eternity.

THE HOLY SPIRIT

I believe that I cannot of my own understanding and strength believe in or come to Jesus Christ, but that the Holy Spirit has called me. He illuminates my soul with many spiritual gifts, and preserves me in the true faith. He also gathers together all Christian people into the Church, so that with one heart and mind they may worship God.

13

Music and dancing

Luther is credited with being the first to ask the question, "Why should the devil have all the best tunes?" He himself composed a number of hymns, including the one here, beautifully translated by Thomas Carlyle. And legend has it that Luther wrote the original version of "Away in a Manger." More surprisingly, he approved of dancing – although, rather endearingly, regretted that his own stern presence would be unwelcome at a dance.

ON DANCING

*D*ancing is for the purpose of teaching courtesy, and of encouraging friendship between young men and girls. At a dance their meeting may be watched to ensure that it is honorable; and once a girl has proved herself responsible at dances, she may be given more freedom. The Pope condemns dancing because he is an enemy of marriage. But let all things be done decently! Let honorable men and matrons be invited to witness everything. I wish I could attend dances myself sometimes, but I fear the merriment would be inhibited by my presence.

ON MUSIC

*M*usic is hateful and intolerable to the devil. I really believe, nor am I ashamed to assert, that next to theology there is no art equal to music. It is the only art, next to theology, that can give a quiet and happy mind, which is manifest proof that the devil, the source of anxiety and sadness, flees from the sound of music as he does from religious worship. That is why the Scriptures are filled with psalms and hymns, in which praise is

given to God. That is why, when we are gathered round God's throne in heaven, we shall sing his glory. Music is the perfect vehicle for expressing our love and devotion to God.

A HYMN

A safe stronghold our God is still
A trusty shield and weapon,
He'll help us clear from all the ill
That hath us now o'ertaken.
The ancient prince of hell
Hath risen with purpose fell;
Strong mail of craft and power
He weareth in this hour
On earth is not his fellow.

With force of arm we nothing can,
Full soon were we down-ridden;
But for us fights the proper Man,
Whom God himself hath bidden.
Ask ye: who is this same?
Christ Jesus is his name,
The Lord Sabaoth's Son;
He, and no other one,
Shall conquer in the battle.

And were this world all devils o'er,
And watching to devour us,
We lay it not to heart so sore;
Not they can overpower us.
And let the prince of ill
Look grim as e'er he will,
He harms us not a whit:
For why? His doom is writ;
A word shall quickly slay him.

God's words, for all their craft and force
One moment will not linger,
But, spite of hell, shall have its course;
Tis written by his finger.
And though they take our life,
Goods, honour, children, wife,
Yet is their profit small:
These things shall vanish all;
The city of God remaineth.

14

Letters to his family

Luther was a tireless correspondent, and naturally his most charming and moving letters are to his family. The picture he paints for his little son Hans of a children's paradise is quite enchanting, if slightly mawkish. And his letters to his wife Kate reveal a deep and robust love.

TO KATE (MARTIN LUTHER'S WIFE) 1536

I apologize for cutting a large hole in Hans's trousers, to supply a patch for my own. The hole was so large that I needed a large patch for it. Trousers seldom fit me well, so when I have a good pair of trousers I need to make them last long. If I were in Italy I know the tailors would be good, so I could simply order new trousers. But in Germany you cannot rely on the tailors, because they make all trousers to a single pattern, regardless of the shape of the person who will wear them. What an eyesore I look when my trousers are too short in the leg and too wide at the stomach! The trouble is that I'm such an odd shape – too tall and too thin.

TO KATE, 1537

Yesterday I left Schmalkalden in the Elector's private carriage. The reason for my leaving is that for three days I have been very unwell, unable to pass water the whole time. I could not rest nor sleep at night nor keep anything in my stomach. In short I felt I was dying, and commended you and our children to God, thinking that I would never see you again. My heart was moved for you, for I thought I was surely in the grave. But men have prayed hard to God, and some even have wept for me before Him, so that He has healed me this night. So thank God for this miracle, and ask the children to do the same. The Elector did everything he could for me, but in vain, And the medicine you have given me did not work. God alone in his mercy could cure me.

15

The death of Magdalene

In 1546, four years before his own death, Luther's daughter Magdalene died. An observer at the bedside wrote the following account.

*A*s his daughter Magdalene lay very ill, Dr. Luther said: "I love her very much, but dear God, if it be your will to take her, I submit to you." Then he said to her as she lay in bed: "Magdalene, my dear daughter, would you like to stay here with your father, or would you willingly go to your Father in heaven?" She answered: "Darling father, as God will." Then he turned away and said: "I love her very much. God has given no one in a thousand years a gift as great as He has given me in her. I am angry with myself that I cannot rejoice in my heart that she shall soon enjoy perfect bliss in heaven."

As Magdalene was dying, her father fell down on his knees beside her bed and wept bitterly, praying that God would release her from her bodily agony. He held her in his arms, and she died with her head on his shoulder.

As they laid her in the coffin, he said: "Darling daughter, you will rise and shine like a star, like the sun even. I am happy for you in spirit, but the flesh is filled with sorrow. The parting grieves me beyond measure. I have sent a saint to heaven."